Freddie     Darla     Chipper     Mr. Chewy

# MR. CHEWY'S BIG ADVENTURE
BY JOHNATHAN RAND

# An AudioCraft Publishing, Inc. book

No part of this publication may be reproduced in whole or in part, or stored in a retrieval system, or transmitted in any form or by any means, electronic, mechanic, photocopying, recording, or otherwise, without written permission from the publisher. For information regarding permission, write to: AudioCraft Publishing, Inc., PO Box 281, Topinabee Island, MI 49791

Freddie Fernortner, Fearless First Grader
#6: Mr. Chewy's Big Adventure
ISBN 1-893699-89-7

Illustrations by Cartoon Studios, Battle Creek, Michigan

Visit www.freddiefernortner.com

Printed in United States of America

First Printing - October 2006

# MR. CHEWY'S
# BIG
# ADVENTURE

# VISIT
# CHILLERMANIA!

## WORLD HEADQUARTERS FOR BOOKS BY JOHNATHAN RAND!

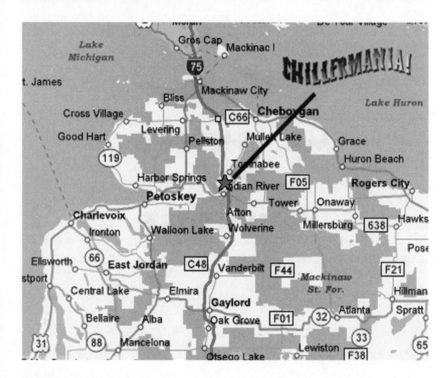

Visit the HOME for books by Johnathan Rand! Featuring books, hats, shirts, bookmarks and other cool stuff not available anywhere else in the world! Plus, watch the American Chillers website for news of special events and signings at **CHILLERMANIA!** with author Johnathan Rand! Located in northern lower Michigan, on I-75! Take exit 313 . . . then south 1 mile!  For more info, call (231) 238-0338. And be afraid! Be veeeery afraaaaaaiiiid . . . .

# 1

"I've got an idea!" Freddie Fernortner said to his two friends, Chipper and Darla.

"Oh, brother," Darla said. "Here we go again."

"Are we going to get into trouble?" Chipper asked.

Freddie shook his head. "Not this time," he said.

However, when Freddie Fernortner said that they wouldn't get into trouble, they usually did.

You see, although Freddie was very smart, he was also very curious . . . and very brave. Once, he and his friends built a flying bicycle. Another time, they visited a haunted house. They even built a giant fort out of old boxes!

One thing was for sure: Freddie and his friends, along with his cat, Mr. Chewy, always had a lot of fun. Mr. Chewy got his name because he likes to chew bubble gum and blow bubbles . . . which was exactly what the cat was doing when Freddie spotted something stuck in a tree.

"Look," Freddie said, pointing. Darla and Chipper turned.

In a tree, not far away, was a kite. It was a big kite, too, and it was very colorful. Its tail was made of rags that had been tied together. A storm had passed through earlier in the day, and Freddie thought someone must have been flying the kite when the string broke.

"That's cool!" Chipper said. "It's the biggest kite I've ever seen in my life!"

Chipper was right. The kite was very big.

"It's pretty," Darla said.

"I'll bet we could get it down," Freddie said.

"But Freddie," Darla said, "how are we going to get it? It's stuck in the tree."

"I can climb up," Freddie said. "It's not very high."

Chipper scratched his head. "I don't know, Freddie," he said. "What happens if you fall?"

"I won't fall," Freddie said. "The kite is stuck on the lowest branch. I could climb up and reach the branch and grab the kite. But I'll need your help."

Not far away, Mr. Chewy sat in the grass, chewing gum. He blew a bubble and it popped. Then, he continued chewing.

"Come on," Freddie said, and the three first graders walked to the tree. Above, the colorful kite fluttered in the breeze.

"How are you going to climb up?" Chipper asked. "There aren't any branches to grab hold of."

"Simple," Freddie said. "You stand next to the tree, Chipper. I'll climb onto your shoulders and reach the branch. Then, I'll climb out and untie the kite."

Darla shook her head. "I don't think it's a good idea, Freddie," she said.

Mr. Chewy, who had followed the three first graders, sat in the grass and blew a bubble.

"Don't worry," Freddie said. "I'll be careful."

Chipper backed up to the tree. In no time at all, Freddie had scrambled up to his friend's shoulders. Then, he reached up and grabbed the branch.

"See?" Freddie said, as he swung his legs up over the branch. "This is easy!"

But as he climbed farther out onto the

limb, it began to bend.

"I hope the branch doesn't break," Chipper said.

"I can't bear to watch," Darla said, covering her eyes with her hands.

"I know!" Freddie said. "Mr. Chewy! Climb up here and help me get the kite!"

Mr. Chewy scampered to the tree and climbed up the trunk. After all, the cat was an expert at climbing trees.

"That's it!" Freddie said, as the cat made his way along the branch. "Climb out past me, and see if you can get the kite unstuck!"

Mr. Chewy seemed to understand, and he climbed past Freddie, walking cautiously along the limb.

On the ground, Chipper watched. Darla peeked through her fingers.

Mr. Chewy approached the kite's tangled tail.

"Good cat!" Freddie said.

The tree limb bent.

"Just a little more," Freddie urged.

The cat took another step.

The branch bent even more.

"Almost there!" Freddie said.

Suddenly, there was a loud cracking sound.

Chipper gasped.

Darla shrieked.

"Oh, no!" Freddie cried.

Without warning, the branch broke, sending Freddie, Mr. Chewy, and the kite falling to the ground!

# 2

It happened so fast there was nothing anyone could do about it.

One moment, Freddie and Mr. Chewy were clinging to a branch in a tree. The next moment, they were tumbling helplessly to the ground.

Freddie landed on his feet, but the branch knocked him to the ground. He was okay, though.

Mr. Chewy, however, wasn't so lucky. The branch knocked him sideways, and the cat landed right on his head!

"Mr. Chewy!" Darla shouted.

The cat got to his feet. He looked dizzy.

"Are you okay, buddy?" Freddie asked. He knelt down next to the cat. Mr. Chewy sat down, shook his head, and looked around. Thankfully, he wasn't hurt.

Freddie reached out and petted his cat on the head. "You're okay," he told Mr. Chewy. "You just bumped your noggin."

Mr. Chewy looked at Freddie. Then, he scampered off.

Freddie stood and looked down at the broken branch on the ground. The kite's tail was still caught in it, but he was easily able to untangle it. When he was finished, he held the kite up.

"Wow!" Chipper said. "It's even bigger than I thought!"

"What are we going to do with it, Freddie?" Darla asked. "Are we going to fly it?"

"You bet!" Freddie said. "I'll bet it'll fly so

high that it will reach the moon!"

"We'll need some new string," Chipper said.

"I have some at home," Darla offered, and she ran to her house.

"This is going to be a blast!" Freddie said. "Let's take it over to the park where there aren't any trees!"

Darla returned a few minutes later, carrying a ball of string. "I don't think there's enough string to reach the moon," she said, "but we might be able to reach the clouds."

Freddie ran home to tell his mother he was going to the park with Chipper and Darla. Mr. Chewy was sitting on the porch.

"Do you want to go to the park, Mr. Chewy?" Freddie asked.

The cat stood and chased after Freddie as he raced back to meet his friends.

"Let's go!" Freddie shouted to Chipper and Darla. Chipper and Freddie picked up the kite and held it carefully while they walked.

Soon, they reached the park. There were only a few other kids playing on the swings. Otherwise, the park was empty.

And the wind was blowing strongly.

"Here," Darla said, handing the ball of string to Freddie.

"Hang on to the kite," Freddie told Chipper, "so the wind doesn't carry it off."

While Chipper held the kite, Freddie carefully tied the string to it. He was careful to tie it well, too, so that it wouldn't untie while they were flying it.

"All set!" Freddie exclaimed.

"This is going to be fun!" Chipper said.

"Yeah," Darla said. "And we won't get into any trouble."

But Darla was wrong . . . because big trouble was only moments away.

# 3

"Is everybody ready?" Freddie asked. He was holding the kite with one hand, and the ball of string with the other. The wind tugged and pulled at the kite, but Freddie held it very tight.

"I'm ready!" Chipper said.

"Me, too!" piped Darla.

Mr. Chewy didn't say anything . . . because he was a cat. He just sat in the grass, beneath a tree, chewing his gum and blowing bubbles. In fact, Mr. Chewy looked quite bored.

"Here we go!" Freddie said, and he let go of the kite. Holding the ball of string in one hand, he began running.

The kite began flying.

Freddie let out some string, and the kite climbed higher into the air, weaving back and forth in the strong wind.

"It's flying! It's flying!" Chipper exclaimed.

"Yay, Freddie!" Darla shouted.

Freddie stopped running, and he turned around. He had a big smile on his face as he watched the kite climb higher and higher into the blue sky.

"This is really cool!" he said. "It's the perfect day to fly a kite!"

But the wind began to die down, and the kite began to fall slowly back to earth.

"Keep it up, Freddie!" Chipper urged.

"Yeah," Darla said. "Keep flying!"

Freddie started running, hoping the kite would catch some air and rise back into the sky.

But the wind died completely, and the kite continued to sink.

All of this, of course, was being watched carefully by Mr. Chewy, who was still sitting beneath the tree. However, when he saw the kite coming down, he saw the colorful tail attached to it. It was wiggling and squirming in the wind, and the cat thought the kite's tail might be a fun toy to play with . . . if he could only catch it in his paws.

The kite continued to fall, and the tail came closer and closer to the ground.

Mr. Chewy sprang. He ran across the green grass lickety-split, heading for the kite's tail, which was, by now, nearly touching the ground.

"Hey, look!" Darla said. "Mr. Chewy is chasing the kite's tail!"

"That's funny!" Chipper said.

"He's kind of cute!" Freddie said.

Mr. Chewy pounced on the kite's tail and held it between his paws. Then, he rolled onto his back and bit into the cloth tail with his teeth.

"He's really having fun!" Darla said.

But something happened that wasn't fun at all. As a matter of fact, it was very, very scary. You see, Mr. Chewy's tail had become wrapped up in the kite's tail . . . and at that very moment, a sudden gust of wind huffed and puffed, sweeping the kite high into the air, taking Mr. Chewy with it!

# 4

Freddie, Darla, and Chipper were shocked. Mr. Chewy was so frightened he nearly spit out his gum!

"Do something, Freddie!" Darla gasped.

Freddie clung tightly to the ball of string, but he had a hard time because the wind was blowing so hard.

Meanwhile, the kite was taking Mr. Chewy even higher into the sky. The poor cat was helpless.

"Pull him in, Freddie!" Chipper said, and Freddie began winding string around the ball, hoping to pull the kite and his cat down to the ground.

"Help me pull the string in!" Freddie shouted. He was very frightened. After all: Mr. Chewy was his friend. He couldn't bear the thought of something bad happening to his cat.

Chipper and Darla raced up to Freddie, and they grabbed the string and started pulling.

"It's working!" Darla said. "We're pulling him down!"

But the wind blew even stronger, and it pulled the string back out. Still, the three friends weren't about to give up, and they pulled the string back in.

The wind blew even harder. High in the sky, clouds were spinning by, pushed by the steady, howling wind.

"I wish it wasn't so windy!" Freddie said in frustration. Just holding the string was hard work, and he wasn't sure if he, Darla, and Chipper could hold on much longer.

Then, disaster struck.

A very strong gust of wind suddenly came up.

Darla, still holding the string, fell to the ground.

Chipper fell, too.

So did Freddie. He looked at the string in his hand. Then, he looked up into the sky at the kite. Mr. Chewy was still dangling from the kite's tail.

"Oh no!" Freddie said. "Oh no!"

"What happened?" Chipper asked.

Freddie held up the kite string. "It broke!" he said. "The kite string broke, and Mr. Chewy is still caught in the kite's tail!"

It was terrible, but it was true.

High in the sky, the blustery wind was sweeping the kite—and Mr. Chewy—away!

# 5

"We've got to save him!" Freddie shouted. "Let's go!" He started to run in the direction the kite and Mr. Chewy were headed.

"But Freddie," Chipper said, "the wind is blowing really hard. We'll never catch up with him!"

"Chipper's right!" Darla said. "Let's get our bikes! We can go faster!"

"Good idea!" Freddie said, and the three friends ran all the way home to get their bikes.

Then, they pedaled as fast as they could back to the park.

But the wind had been blowing a great deal. It roared through the trees, pulling leaves from their branches. It howled at the three friends' ears, and tossed their hair wildly about.

Worst of all, there was no sign of Mr. Chewy. The wind had taken him away.

Freddie, Chipper, and Darla sat on their bikes, looking into the sky, hoping to catch a glimpse of the wayward kite and the helpless cat.

"This is all my fault," Freddie said. He was very sad, and he was very scared. Mr. Chewy was a good friend, and he couldn't bear thinking that the wind and the kite had carried the cat away . . . maybe forever.

"Don't worry, Freddie," Darla said. "We'll find him."

"Yeah," Chipper said. "He's our friend, too. We'll find him, even if we have to look forever!"

All of a sudden, Freddie spotted something.

Something in the air.

Something colorful.

And that something colorful had a long tail . . . and at the end of that tail was Mr. Chewy!

"There he is!" Freddie pointed. "He's way over there!"

"Uh-oh!" Chipper said. "Look where he's headed!"

Freddie gasped.

Darla shrieked.

Chipper covered his eyes with his hands.

*Mr. Chewy was headed straight for the water tower!*

# 6

At the very last second, just as it appeared that Mr. Chewy was going to hit the water tower, the wind changed direction, taking the kite and the cat out of danger.

The three friends let out sighs of relief.

"Wow," Darla said. "Mr. Chewy was really lucky, that time!"

"Yeah, but he's still in trouble," Freddie said. "We've got to save him. Come on!"

And with that, Freddie, Chipper, and Darla

took off on their bikes, riding as fast as they could down the sidewalk, heading toward the kite and Mr. Chewy.

"But what are we going to do, Freddie?" Chipper panted as he pedaled his bike as fast as he could.

"I don't know!" Freddie replied as the wind whipped at his face. "But we've got to do something! Hang in there, Mr. Chewy!" he called up into the sky.

Of course, Mr. Chewy was much too far away to hear Freddie call out, but it made Freddie feel better, just the same.

"Wait, Freddie," Darla said. She slowed her bike to a stop and pointed up into the sky. "The wind has changed direction again. It's bringing the kite and Mr. Chewy back over the park!"

"Let's get back there!" Freddie exclaimed. "If the wind dies down, maybe we can catch him!"

The three turned their bikes around and

headed back to the park. Sure enough, the kite and Mr. Chewy were there . . . but they were still high in the sky, carried by a furious wind.

"What now?" Chipper asked.

"We have to watch him carefully," Freddie said. "This wind can't keep blowing like it is. When it lets up, the kite and Mr. Chewy will come down. We have to be there when that happens!"

The kite, with Mr. Chewy still tied to its tail, was now directly above Freddie, Chipper, and Darla . . . but not for long.

Because the wind changed again.

"He's being carried away again, Freddie!" Darla shouted as she pointed up into the air. "Now, he's going the other way!"

Which was not good news. The wind was carrying the kite and the cat past the park . . . right over a small lake.

And that's where, without any warning at all, the wind slowed.

"Thank goodness!" Darla said. "Look! Mr. Chewy is coming back to the ground!"

"No, he's not!" Freddie replied. He sounded scared . . . and with very good reason. Because the kite and the cat were, indeed, falling slowly.

That wasn't the problem.

The problem was that the kite and Mr. Chewy were going to splash down in the lake.

"Mr. Chewy can't swim!" Freddie gasped.

But there was nothing the three friends could do but watch helplessly as kite and cat fell down, down, toward the lake.

# 7

This time, all three friends covered their eyes with their hands. They couldn't bear to watch Mr. Chewy land helplessly in the water. They waited for the splash that would tell them the kite and cat had touched down.

Then, it would be all over for the kite, and their good pal, Mr. Chewy.

But the splash never came.

They waited, hands covering their eyes.

No splash.

Freddie was the first to peek through his fingers.

"Look!" he exclaimed. "The wind changed again! Mr. Chewy is safe!"

Freddie and Darla pulled their hands from their faces so they could see. True to Freddie's words, the wind had shifted again. This time, it had lifted the kite and Mr. Chewy back up into the sky. They were drifting away from the lake.

"I guess it's true what they say about cats having nine lives," Chipper said.

"Yeah," Freddie agreed, "but I hope Mr. Chewy doesn't use all of his up in one day!"

Darla pointed. "Look, Freddie," she said. "The wind is taking Mr. Chewy back toward your house!"

"Let's go!" Freddie said, and, once again, the three friends turned their bikes around and sped off, in yet another desperate attempt to save their good pal, Mr. Chewy.

All the while, the wind blew, and blew, and

blew. And all the while, it carried the kite and the cat farther and farther away.

But finally, there was good news coming. The wind, even though it was very strong, was dying down. Which meant the kite and Mr. Chewy were slowly lowering back to the ground.

Freddie, Chipper, and Darla continued pedaling, careful to watch where they were going, but also careful to keep an eye to the sky.

"He's coming down!" Chipper exclaimed. "He's coming down, right on our block! And he's coming down slow!"

That was good news. It meant that, hopefully, Mr. Chewy would have a soft, safe landing.

But here's where trouble came, and in a big way.

You see, Freddie, Chipper, and Darla weren't the only ones chasing Mr. Chewy. The three first graders didn't know it yet, but there were others in the neighborhood who had been watching the cat high in the sky . . . and they, too, were waiting for Mr. Chewy to come back to earth.

Can you guess who else was chasing after Mr. Chewy?

You're right.

Dogs. Three of them, exactly.

And from the looks of it, the dogs were going to reach Mr. Chewy first!

# 8

Freddie, Chipper, and Darla didn't know anything was wrong. They certainly didn't know any dogs were around . . . until three of them went flying past them, barking and yelping, in hot pursuit of Mr. Chewy.

Of course, the kite and Mr. Chewy were still in the air, but they were coming down slowly. And that meant the dogs would reach the cat before Freddie, Chipper, and Darla!

"We've got to pedal faster!" Freddie urged.

"If Mr. Chewy comes down to the ground and those dogs get there first, he'll be a goner!"

"We won't let it happen, Freddie!" Chipper said, pedaling faster. "I promise!"

On and on they pedaled, down the block, following the three dogs who were chasing the flying cat. Several neighbors peered out their windows to see what all the fuss and barking was about. Everyone gasped at the sight of the poor cat being carried in the air by the kite and the wind.

"We're catching up to the dogs!" Darla said. The three first graders were really pedaling now, and the dogs weren't far in front of them. The kite and Mr. Chewy, however, were still in the air, being carried by a firm, brisk wind.

"Uh-oh, Freddie," Chipper said. "I think I see another problem."

"What?" Freddie asked as the three continued pedaling.

"Up ahead!" Chipper said. "The kite and Mr. Chewy are coming down . . . but he's headed right for the top of that tree!"

Freddie suddenly saw the tree Chipper was talking about. He realized his friend was right: Mr. Chewy and the kite were in danger of crashing into the top of a large tree!

"This is terrible!" Darla exclaimed.

Darla was right. It really *was* terrible. So far, Mr. Chewy had been very, very lucky.

But it looked like his luck had just ran out. Freddie, Darla, and Chipper could do nothing but watch as a gust of wind pushed the kite and Mr. Chewy right into the tip-top branches of a huge tree!

# 9

Things weren't looking good.

Oh, there was *one* good thing, and that was the fact that Mr. Chewy was no longer flying high in the sky, tied to the tail of a kite. But now he was stuck in the top of a tree, dangling by the kite's tail . . . and there were three dogs that wanted him very badly!

Freddie, Chipper, and Darla stopped their bikes at the bottom of the tree. The dogs were yapping and yelping, looking up at Mr. Chewy, high in the tree.

"Are you okay, Mr. Chewy?" Freddie called out.

Mr. Chewy blew a bubble. It popped, and he kept on chewing.

"What do we do, Freddie?" Darla asked. She was worried. If Mr. Chewy fell, he'd be in more trouble than he was already in.

"Let's try to get the dogs to go home," Freddie said.

"Shoo!" Chipper said gruffly. He waved his arms, trying to get the dogs to leave.

"Go home!" Darla ordered. "Go home right now!"

The dogs paid no attention to the three first graders. They continued to bark and yelp at the helpless cat dangling from the top of the tree.

"Go on, get out of here!" Chipper ordered. "Don't you guys have a bone to dig up somewhere? Go on! Go home!"

Suddenly, Darla's eyes grew wide. "Hey, guys!" she exclaimed. "I have an idea! It's a really,

really good one, too!"

"What is it?" Freddie asked.

And when Darla explained her idea, Freddie and Chipper realized that it just might work . . . but they would have to act fast!

# 10

Freddie looked up. "Don't worry, buddy!" he told Mr. Chewy, who was still at the very top of the tree. "Darla has a plan! Stay right where you are, and we'll be right back!"

This was Darla's plan:

The three of them would bicycle to a nearby store and buy a bag of dog treats. Then, they would race back to the tree, and create a trail of dog treats leading away from the tree. The dogs would gobble up the treats, and soon they would be far from the tree! Mr. Chewy would be able to come down safely without worrying!

The three friends hopped onto their bikes and rode to the corner store a few blocks away.

"How much do dog treats cost?" Chipper asked as they wandered down the pet food aisle.

Freddie shrugged. "I don't know," he said, shaking his head. "I've never bought dog treats before."

"I hope we have enough money," Darla said.

As it turned out, the three had just enough money to buy a box of treats called Woof-Woof Biscuits.

"That sure is a funny name for a dog treat," Chipper said, reading the box.

"Hey, if the dogs like the treats, that's all that matters," Freddie said.

They paid for the box of treats. Soon, they were back on their bikes, racing to the tree, the three dogs, and Mr. Chewy. High above, Mr.

Chewy was still at the top of the tree. He looked very scared.

You would be, too, if you were a cat in a tree with three dogs waiting for you to come down!

"Hey, poochy-woochy," Freddie said, opening the box of Woof-Woof Biscuits. "Come and get it!"

He pulled out a biscuit and held it out for the dogs to see. At first, the dogs didn't pay much attention. But when they picked up the scent of the biscuits, they suddenly lost all interest in the cat in the tree.

"That's it," Freddie said, giving each of the dogs a biscuit. "That's it. Come away from the tree." He threw several biscuits, and the dogs charged after them.

"They like them!" Darla said. "It's going to work!"

"Here, Darla," Freddie said, and he handed her the box of Woof-Woof Biscuits. "Lead the dogs away with the treats, so Mr. Chewy can climb down."

Darla took the box and backed away. The dogs followed her eagerly, waiting for the next handout. She continued walking away, all the while dropping Woof-Woof Biscuits on the ground. The dogs followed, and soon, they, along with Darla, were out of sight.

Freddie looked up. "It's safe now, Mr. Chewy!" he hollered. "You can come down now!"

But Mr. Chewy didn't move.

"Come on, buddy!" Freddie called again. "The dogs are gone. You'll be safe. I promise."

"Maybe he can't come down," Chipper said. "Maybe he's stuck."

Freddie looked closer . . . and what he saw was not good news at all.

Mr. Chewy's tail was still wrapped in the kite's tail. That meant if Mr. Chewy was going to come down, then someone would have to go up and help him.

And, being that Mr. Chewy was Freddie's cat, and Freddie loved his cat very much, it was only right that Freddie be the one to climb the tree.

The good news was: Freddie was an very good tree climber.

The bad news was: there was something in the tree that Freddie had no way of knowing was there.

Something that could be very scary, indeed.

Freddie grabbed a branch and began climbing . . . unaware of the danger he was about to face.

# 11

Now, it's true that Freddie Fernortner was a good tree climber. But he knew he had to be very, very careful. After all . . . he didn't want to fall down and get hurt! So, as he climbed, he went very slowly.

Meanwhile, Darla had returned.

"I don't think we'll be seeing those dogs for a while," she said. "I fed them all of the Woof-Woof Biscuits." But when she saw Freddie climbing the tree, she gasped.

"What's Freddie doing?!?!" she exclaimed.

"Mr. Chewy's tail is still caught in the kite's tail," Chipper explained. "Freddie has to climb up to help him."

"I hope he's careful," Darla said.

"Oh, he'll be careful," Chipper replied. "He's fearless . . . but he's not careless."

Limb by limb, branch by branch, Freddie climbed the tree. Once in a while, he would look down and wave at Chipper and Darla, to let them know he was okay.

And he talked to Mr. Chewy as he climbed.

"Hang on, pal," he said. "I'm almost there. Don't go anywhere."

Which was a silly thing to say. After all: Mr. Chewy's tail was still tied to the kite's tail. He wasn't going anywhere!

"You're halfway there, Freddie!" Chipper shouted up to him.

"Yeah, you're doing great!" Darla exclaimed.

"I'll have Mr. Chewy safe on the ground in no time at all!" Freddie called down to them. Then, he looked up at Mr. Chewy, who was blowing a bubble at that very moment. "Almost there, Mr. Chewy," Freddie said. "Just a few more branches."

Freddie could see Mr. Chewy. He could see the kite, caught in the branches at the top of the tree. He could see its tail, knotted up around his cat's tail.

What he could *not* see was the beehive, hanging on a branch on the other side of the tree . . . until it was too late.

# 12

There was a buzzing sound around Freddie's ear. At first, he thought it was a mosquito, and he was about to wave his arm to swipe the insect away.

Before he did, however, something landed on his arm . . . something that was *not* a mosquito!

"Uh-oh," Freddie said, and he stopped moving. The bee was walking on his arm, and it looked angry.

Still, Freddie didn't move. He didn't want the bee to sting him.

Another bee landed, and another. Then another. Freddie looked around, and that's when he saw it: on a branch, not far away, was a beehive. He'd come a little too close, and the bees were wondering what he was up to.

"Please, bees!" Freddie pleaded. "I'm only trying to save my cat! Please don't sting me!"

The bees on his arm thought about this for a moment. They buzzed among themselves, then looked at Freddie warily.

"I promise," Freddie continued. "I just want to climb up and rescue my cat. I don't want to hurt you or your hive."

Again, the bees on his arm buzzed to one another. Then, they looked at Freddie, and then up at Mr. Chewy, who was still dangling at the top of the tree.

The bees decided Freddie meant them no harm. They buzzed into the air and flew off, getting back to the busy work that all bees do.

Freddie let out a sigh of relief. "That was a

close one," he breathed.

"Are you all right, Freddie?" Darla called up. She and Chipper saw Freddie frozen in the tree, but they were too far away to see the bees.

"I am, now!" Freddie called down to them. "There is a beehive up here, but they won't bother me if I don't bother them."

"Wow," Darla said to Chipper. "Freddie was really lucky."

"Yeah," Chipper replied. "It's a good thing Freddie knows what he's doing."

Freddie continued to climb. Finally, he reached the top of the tree where Mr. Chewy dangled.

"This will take just a second, Mr. Chewy," Freddie said. With one arm, he held onto a branch, and with the other, he carefully picked up his cat and placed him on his shoulder.

"Stay right there, buddy," Freddie said, and he began untangling the kite's tail from Mr. Chewy's tail.

"Got it!" he said, and Mr. Chewy licked Freddie's cheek. His tongue felt like sandpaper.

"You hang on tight, Mr. Chewy," Freddie told his cat, "and I'll have us safe and sound on the ground in a jiffy!"

True, Freddie would have his cat back on the ground in a jiffy.

The problem was that the cat *still* wasn't going to be safe . . . because they'd forgotten all about something very important.

And they were about to find out what it was.

# 13

Very carefully, Freddie began to climb back down the tree. It was a bit harder this time, because he needed one arm to hold Mr. Chewy.

And when he neared the beehive, he was careful to stay as far away as possible. A few bees buzzed around, but they left him alone.

"You're doing great, Freddie!" Chipper shouted.

"Yeah!" Darla said. "You're almost on the ground."

Down, down, Freddie climbed, holding Mr. Chewy with one arm, and using the other arm to grasp branches.

Finally, Freddie's feet touched the ground. Darla threw her arms around Mr. Chewy and Freddie and gave them both a big hug. Chipper wrapped his arms around all of them. They were all very, very glad that Mr. Chewy's terrible ordeal was over.

Freddie placed Mr. Chewy on the ground. "I'll bet you're happy to have all four paws on the ground, aren't you, Mr. Chewy?"

The cat meowed happily, then blew a bubble. The bubble popped, and pink gum went all over his whiskers.

Freddie, Darla, and Chipper laughed. They laughed and laughed and laughed. It had been a scary day for all of them . . . but it was over now. Mr. Chewy was safe.

But was he?

The three first graders were laughing so

hard they didn't hear the sound of dogs barking, until it was already too late.

A dog suddenly appeared, followed by another one. And another one!

But before Freddie could pick up Mr. Chewy, the cat had already made a decision to flee.

The chase was on! But who was faster: the dogs . . . or Mr. Chewy?

Freddie, Chipper, and Darla would find out, very soon . . . .

# 14

Mr. Chewy fled, running as fast as his little paws could take him.

The dogs sped by, running as fast as their big paws could take them.

"Oh, no!" Freddie said. "Come on, guys! We've got to save Mr. Chewy again!"

They hopped on their bicycles and joined the chase. It actually looked quite funny: a single cat, racing across the lawn, followed by three eager dogs and three first graders on bicycles.

But it wouldn't be funny if the dogs reached Mr. Chewy before he could get away!

"Mr. Chewy!" Freddie cried out as he pedaled his bike as fast as he could. "Climb up into a tree! Climb up into a tree!"

"But Freddie," Chipper huffed as he pedaled, "you just got him *out* of a tree!"

"Mr. Chewy knows how to climb trees!" Freddie replied. "He just can't climb when his tail is caught."

"There's a tree, right over there!" Darla said. "Maybe Mr. Chewy can make it there in time!"

Mr. Chewy had already spotted the tree, and was heading right for it. The dogs, however, were very fast, and they were only a few feet behind the speeding cat.

"Go, Mr. Chewy, go!" Freddie shouted.

Suddenly, one of the dogs leapt.

"I can't bear to watch!" Darla shrieked.

"Jump, Mr. Chewy, jump!" Freddie

hollered.

At the last second, right before the dog pounced, Mr. Chewy leapt. He sprang up, leaping as high as he could, landing on a low branch in the tree . . . just out of reach of the frantic dogs. Just to be safe, however, Mr. Chewy leapt up one more branch.

Below, on the ground, the dogs yipped and yapped and ran around in circles. They jumped and barked, but there was nothing they could do. Mr. Chewy was safely perched on a low tree branch, and he wasn't coming down. He blew a bubble and looked down at the three dogs as if he could care less about them.

The three first graders leapt from their bikes and raced to the tree.

"You guys go home!" Freddie ordered the dogs. "Leave my cat alone!"

The dogs wouldn't leave. They just kept barking and running around in circles, looking up at Mr. Chewy.

"What are we going to do?" Darla asked. "We don't have any more Woof-Woof Biscuits."

"And we don't have the money to buy any more," Chipper said glumly.

"Wait," Freddie said, stroking his chin with his thumb and finger. "Maybe we could try something else."

"Like what?" Darla asked.

"Yeah," Chipper chimed. "What are you thinking, Freddie?"

"You guys wait right here and keep an eye on Mr. Chewy," Freddie said. "I'll be right back!"

What was Freddie's big idea? How was he going to save Mr. Chewy from the three dogs?

Darla didn't know.

Chipper didn't know.

Even Mr. Chewy didn't know.

But Freddie knew. Question was: would his idea work?

He'd find out soon enough!

# 15

Freddie hopped on his bike and sped madly away.

"What do you think he's going to do?" Chipper asked.

Darla shrugged. "I don't know," Darla replied, "I just hope he knows what he's doing."

The dogs continued to bark wildly. Mr. Chewy continued to sit on the tree branch, looking down, chewing his bubble gum.

Minutes ticked passed. The dogs continued

their frantic barking and yelping.

Chipper suddenly pointed. "Here comes Freddie!" he exclaimed.

Darla turned to see Freddie pedaling wildly toward them. He was carrying something beneath his arm, but Chipper and Darla couldn't tell what it was.

"I've got it!" Freddie said as he skidded his bike to a halt. He leapt off and held up a large, paper grocery sack that he'd rolled up and carried beneath his arm.

"A paper bag?" Chipper said, scratching his head. "What are you going to do with that?"

Darla was confused, too. "Yeah, Freddie," she said, "what are you going to do with a paper bag?"

"Watch," Freddie said, and he unrolled the paper bag and reached his arm inside, pulling out a single hamburger patty.

"It was left over from dinner last night," he said. "It was in the fridge."

"But Freddie," Darla said, "what are you going to do with it?"

Freddie didn't answer. Instead, he walked over to the three dogs beneath the tree, carrying the bag in one hand and the hamburger patty in the other.

At first, the dogs didn't pay any attention to him.

But when they got a whiff of the hamburger patty, all three suddenly stopped barking. Their ears went up, and they sat down, looking at the hamburger patty in Freddie's hand. All three dogs licked their lips.

*"Oh, I get it,"* Chipper whispered. *"It's the old hamburger-patty-grocery-bag trick."*

*"What's that?"* Darla whispered back.

Chipper shrugged. *"I don't know,"* he replied. *"But I'm sure Freddie does."*

"Look at what I've got," Freddie said to the dogs as he waved the hamburger patty in the air. "It's a hamburger. My mom made it, so you know it's really good."

The dogs nodded their heads. Everyone knew Mrs. Fernortner was a very good cook.

"Would you like this hamburger?" Freddie asked the dogs.

They wagged their tails.

Freddie tucked the paper bag beneath his arm and carefully broke the hamburger patty into three pieces. Then, he threw them as far as he could!

The dogs instantly sprang . . . and so did Freddie. He opened up the paper sack and ran up to the tree.

"Jump, Mr. Chewy, jump!" he exclaimed. "Jump into the bag!"

Mr. Chewy leapt from his perch on the branch, and Freddie caught him inside the bag. Then, he folded the top of the bag over . . . just as the dogs returned. They had already gobbled up the hamburger snacks, and were returning to wait for the cat.

Freddie walked back to where Darla and Chipper stood, carrying the sack.

"That was sneaky!" Chipper said.

"Yeah, Freddie!" Darla giggled. "You sure fooled them!"

The dogs were beneath the tree, looking up. All three seemed very confused, because they didn't know where the cat had gone.

"Let's go," Freddie said, "before they figure out what's going on."

The three first graders hopped on their bikes. Freddie, being very careful, carried the bag containing Mr. Chewy beneath his arm. He was also careful as he pedaled, until they'd reached his house. Then, he stopped his bike, got off, walked to the porch, and let the cat out of the bag.

Chipper and Darla joined him, and the three friends petted the cat, scratching him behind his ears and rubbing his belly. Freddie went inside and returned with a brand new stick of gum for Mr. Chewy.

"Wow," Darla said. "I'm glad that adventure is over. That was scary!"

"Imagine how Mr. Chewy felt," Freddie said.

"All's well that ends well," Chipper said.

"What's that mean?" Darla asked.

Chipper scratched his head. "I'm not sure. But my dad says it all the time."

"Speaking of 'Dads'," Freddie said, "here comes my dad, right now."

Mr. Fernorter's big car was pulling into the driveway. He parked the car and got out.

"Hi, Mr. Fernortner!" both Darla and Chipper said.

"Hello, kids; hello, Freddie," Mr. Fernortner replied. "Did you have fun today?"

"Sort of," Freddie said.

"Well, I've got something for you, and I think it'll be a *lot* of fun."

Mr. Fernortner pulled a big box from the back seat. "This is for you guys," he said, placing the box on the ground.

Freddie, Chipper, and Darla walked over to the box. There were big, bold letters on its side that read:

**CONTAINS ONE
MAGICAL WADING POOL**

"A magical wading pool!" Freddie exclaimed, and the three first graders began jumping up and down and carrying on with cheers of delight. Mr. Fernortner laughed, and went into the house.

"This is going to be so much fun!" Freddie exclaimed. "I've never had a magical wading pool!"

"Me neither!" Chipper said.

"I never knew they made magical wading pools," Darla said.

"Let's open it up!" Freddie said with a wide grin, and the three friends began tearing into the box.

Another wild, zany adventure was about to begin for Freddie Fernortner, Fearless First Grader.

**NEXT:**

**FREDDIE FERNORTNER,**

**FEARLESS FIRST GRADER**

**BOOK SEVEN:**

**THE MAGICAL WADING POOL**

**CONTINUE ON TO READ**

**THE FIRST THREE CHAPTERS**

**FOR FREE!**

# 1

The day Freddie Fernortner's father brought home the magical wading pool was an exciting day, indeed. You see, Freddie, along with his best friends Darla and Chipper, had already had one big adventure: they had to save Freddie's cat, Mr. Chewy, from being carried away by a kite! Mr. Chewy got his name because, as a kitten, he learned how to chew gum and blow bubbles. And if you ever saw a cat chew gum and blow bubbles, you know just how funny it is!

The three first graders (and Freddie's cat, of course) were always looking for exciting things to do. Freddie Fernortner was very smart, and very fearless . . . which sometimes got the three friends in a lot of trouble.

And, once again, trouble wasn't far away.

Freddie, Darla, Chipper, and Mr. Chewy had been sitting on Freddie's porch when Mr. Fernortner came home carrying a box with bold letters that read:

## CONTAINS ONE
## MAGICAL WADING POOL

The three friends wasted no time tearing into the box to see what it was all about.

"A magical wading pool!" Freddie exclaimed. "I wonder what it does!"

"I don't know," Chipper said as he helped tear into the box. "But I bet it'll be fun!"

Inside the box were several items, including

a blue inflatable pool, masks, and some strange looking, colorful rubber tubes. Darla picked one up and looked at it.

"What this?" she wondered aloud.

"That's a snorkel," Freddie replied. "You use it to breathe while you float on the surface of the water. That way, you can look down through your mask and not have to take your face out of the water."

"It will be cool to have our very own pool to swim in!" Chipper said.

"Let's set it up in my back yard," Freddie said. "Come on. Let's put all this stuff back in the box and carry it around back."

The three first graders returned the masks and snorkels to the box. Then, they carefully placed the limp plastic pool inside, too. (Actually, it didn't look anything at all like a pool . . . not yet, anyway.)

All the while, Mr. Chewy watched from the porch, chewing gum and blowing bubbles.

The box wasn't very heavy, and the three friends had no trouble at all carrying it into the back yard. Now, all they had to do was find the perfect spot.

"I say we set it up over there," Freddie said as he pointed, "near the bird bath. That's a good, sunny spot."

"Sounds good to me," Chipper said.

"Me, too," chimed Darla.

They carried the big box into the yard next to the bird bath. The day was sunny and bright. The wind had been blowing earlier, and it had been quite gusty. Now, however, there was hardly any wind at all.

Chipper looked around. "Hey, Freddie," he said, "remember when we built that big box fort? That was a lot of fun!"

Freddie laughed. "Yeah," he said. "We should do that again sometime!"

Suddenly, Mrs. Fernortner's voice called out from the house. "Freddie! Time for dinner!"

"Okay, Mom," he replied. He was hungry . . . but he was a little disappointed. After all . . . he wanted to get right to work, setting up the magical wading pool.

"I guess we'll have to wait until tomorrow to set up our magical wading pool," he said. "Let's meet here in the morning. Don't forget to wear your swim suit!"

"I don't get it," Darla said as she gazed at the pool. She had a puzzled look on her face. "What's so magical about it?"

It was a good question. Just what was so magical about the pool? Was it even magical at all?

Oh, you can bet it was . . . and Freddie, Darla, and Chipper would find out for themselves the very next day!

# 2

The next day was sunny, bright, and warm. The sky was a beautiful blue, and there were no clouds. The flowers in Mrs. Fernortner's garden soaked up the sunshine, while bumblebees flitted among the colorful petals.

Freddie, Chipper, and Darla met in Freddie's back yard. Mr. Chewy was there, too, and he sat by the bird bath, watching the three first graders. And, as usual, the cat was chewing gum and blowing bubbles.

"I was so excited last night I could hardly sleep!" Freddie said.

"Me, too!" Chipper said. "I've never been in a magical wading pool!"

The three first graders began to assemble the pool . . . which was pretty easy. All they had to do was take it out of the box (it looked like a big, blue bag that was folded) and blow it up. Freddie, Chipper, and Darla each took turns. Soon, the wading pool was ready. There was just one more thing they needed to do.

"Chipper, go get the hose from my mom's flower garden," Freddie said. "All we have to do is fill the pool with water, and we'll be ready."

Chipper hustled over to Mrs. Fernortner's garden and found the bright green water hose. He picked it up and carried it to the empty pool. While he did, Freddie ran to the house and turned the water on. Then, he ran back to the pool, where Darla and Chipper waited.

Water began running from the hose, and

Freddie placed the end of it inside the wading pool. The water swirled and splashed as it filled the small wading pool.

But there was one small problem, and Darla was the first to notice it.

"The pool is very small, Freddie," she said. "How are the three of us going to fit inside? If we try to swim, there won't be hardly any room."

Chipper scratched his head. "Gee, Freddie," he said. "Darla is right. The pool *is* really small."

Freddie agreed. "Yeah, it's small," he said. "But it will still be a lot of fun. And besides . . . the box says that it's magical."

"I haven't seen anything magical, yet," Darla said.

"Me neither," Chipper said.

True, the pool didn't look magical. There were no colorful decorations of fish or shells or anything. It was just a bright, plain blue.

In a few minutes, the pool was filled with

water. Freddie ran back to the side of the house and turned the water off. Then he ran back to the pool. Darla and Chipper were staring down into the clean, clear water.

"It still doesn't look very magical," Darla said.

"Well, we have to give it a chance," Freddie said. And with that, he placed his foot in the water.

"Yipes!" he said, pulling his foot out quickly. "It's ice cold!"

Darla tried with her foot, and she, too, pulled it out really fast. "You're right, Freddie," she said with a shiver. "It's freezing!"

"Let's wait for a while until the sun warms it up," Freddie said. "We'll freeze if we try and swim right now!"

The three first graders agreed to meet after lunch, in Freddie's back yard. That would give the sun plenty of time to warm the water in the magical wading pool.

"Very strange," Freddie said as he looked at the pool after Chipper and Darla had left. Mr. Chewy was still near the bird bath, chewing gum and blowing bubbles, but now he scampered up to the edge of the pool and looked into the water.

"It says it's a magical wading pool, Mr. Chewy," he said to his cat, "but it looks just like an ordinary wading pool."

But he was still excited about trying it out. That is, of course, when the water warmed up.

So, he went inside, where it was soon time for lunch. His mother made him a peanut butter and jelly sandwich. She also gave him an apple, several carrot sticks, and a glass of milk. She placed the meal on a tray, and Freddie carried it outside to the back yard patio, where he sat at the picnic table and ate. When he was finished, he took the tray back to the kitchen, thanked his mother, and went back outside. He sat down beneath a tree and waited for Darla and Chipper to arrive.

And, although Freddie didn't know it yet, the tiny wading pool was hard at work, becoming more and more magical by the moment.

# 3

"Freddie! Hey Freddie! Are you ready?"

It was Chipper. He was running across the grass, barefoot. Darla wasn't far behind him. Both children carried colorful beach towels.

Freddie stood. "Yeah!" he exclaimed. "Let's go!"

He got up, and the three first graders

walked to the edge of the pool. Mr. Chewy had been sitting by Mrs. Fernortner's flower garden, watching bumblebees, and he, too, joined the children at the wading pool.

"Let's not forget the masks and snorkels," Chipper said.

Freddie went to the box and turned it upside down. Out came four masks and four snorkels.

"That's funny," Darla said. "There's a mask and snorkel for each of us, and one extra."

"Maybe Mr. Chewy would like to go," Chipper snickered.

"Hey, maybe he would!" Freddie said. Then he turned to Mr. Chewy. "Do you want to swim in the magical wading pool?"

he asked.

"But Freddie," Darla interrupted, "Mr. Chewy can't swim."

"The pool is only a few inches deep," Freddie said. "He won't need to swim. He can just wade around with us."

Mr. Chewy seemed to like this idea. He scampered over to Mrs. Fernortner's garden, where he quickly dug a small hole in the dirt. He placed his wad of gum in the hole, then covered it up. (If Mrs. Fernortner knew he was doing this, she would not be very happy.) Then he ambled back to the waiting first graders.

"Let's see if this mask will fit you, Mr. Chewy," Freddie said. He slipped the mask over the cat's head. Amazingly, it was a perfect fit.

Darla laughed. "He looks funny!" she said as Freddie affixed the snorkel to Mr. Chewy's mask.

Then, the three first graders each put on a mask and clipped a snorkel to the strap.

"See, you put this end of the snorkel in your mouth, like this," Freddie said, showing Chipper and Darla. When he put it in his mouth is was hard for him to talk, but he managed. "That's how we can breathe while we look down in the water."

Chipper and Darla each put their snorkels into their mouths.

"I'm ready!" Chipper said, and his voice sounded hollow in the snorkel.

"I'm ready, too!" Darla said.

"We sound funny," Chipper said with

a laugh. Mr. Chewy meowed in the snorkel, and he, too, sounded funny.

"Then, let's go!" Freddie said, placing a foot in the wading pool. The water was only deep enough to come up to his shin.

Then, he stepped all the way inside, and stood.

Darla stepped into the pool, and Chipper followed. Then, Mr. Chewy made a single, short leap . . . and landed in the pool. The water came up to his neck, but he didn't mind at all.

"So, where's the magic?" Chipper asked.

"I'm not feeling very magical," Darla said. "Maybe we got a broken wading pool."

"Maybe we have to swim around,"

Freddie said.

"Gee, there's not much room, with the three of us and Mr. Chewy," Chipper said.

"Well, let's give it a try," Freddie said, and he knelt down into the cool water.

Darla and Chipper knelt down, too.

"Just put your face in the water and breathe through your snorkel," Freddie said.

At the exact same time, the three first graders and Mr. Chewy leaned forward and placed their face masks into the water—and what they saw was *incredible*.

# WATCH FOR MORE FREDDIE FERNORTNER, FEARLESS FIRST GRADER BOOKS, COMING SOON!